Ruffling Feathers

Louise Bretland-Treharne

ICONAU

Published by Iconau
Northcliff
Ferryside
SA17 5RS
www.iconau.com

First published in 2022
re-printed February 2023
© Louise Bretland-Treharne
All rights reserved

ISBN 978-1-907476-37-2

edited by Mel Perry
typeset in calibri by iconau.com
printed and bound by proprint-wales.co.uk
cover collage by Louise Bretland-Treharne
design Dominic Williams

British Library Cataloguing in Publication data
A cataloguing record for this book is available from the
British Library.

Valuing all of creation. All people, animals, and life matters. Care a word celebrated, with some caution and concern. Opportunities for us all in taking turns to care.

Poems

As a Naughty Adult

As a naughty adult of playfulness my
message to us all
is hold on trustingly to the anchor of
kindness.
Keep believing in the power of blessings.
Any lack has an opposite polarity, so be in
ease
within the temporary pit stop.
For goodness' sake never stop laughing
whether silently or loudly!

Bloody Dangerous

Pale faced Martin's intrusion.
A serious proper jam and toast moment.
Posh I was, lap clad with thick serviette of quality.
"What Martin?"
"Women's shower room," says Martin, "is holder of a flaming dangerous hairdryer!"
"Martin, there's no hairdryer in showering area."
"Yes there is," blurts Martin.

Tossing thoughts, requiring a priority decision.
Toast and jam continued consumption, or, a mysterious hairdryer investigation?
"Martin, show me" I suggested.
My speedy long legs come second place, as Martin's lengthy strides overtake.

Hatch opened, flames roar!
Dirty uncontrollable laughter, I can't contain.
Pelvic muscles clenching moment, to keep at bay my pee.
Womanhood of willingness at 17, no

guarantees to prevent
pelvic dam failure!
No arm bands at hand, just in case of deep
pool experience.
All is well as leaky eyes from laughter, the
only wet experience.

High pitched testosterone-lack moment, as
Martin shrieks, "Not funny"
His out-of-control diaphragm wobbles
from exasperation.
This made worse by shallow breathing, with
inadequately air-filled
lungs, which leaves an interesting vocal
offering from Martin.

Dear friend's face of perplexed anguish,
looks in my direction, with anticipation of
my reply. More belly aching laughter, with
further pelvic floor clenching.

"Martin, that's the sanitary towels
incinerator."
The cogs within Martin's head manically
turn.
A gasp, as if punched in the gut from my
friend.

Realisation moment as Martin clicks that this thing of mystery, is within realms of women's private bits.

In those days this period business hush, hush, to be shared with women only. Women would refer to menstruation in whispers, as if sharing a dirty secret.

No sisters has Martin but a mother yes, but that another level! Martin's virginal reality of innocence knows women as friends only. A totally respectful place of women's bits Martin's reality, as not explored or shared, as yet!

2020 WhatsApp photo and message says; Guess what Martin? Let this photo cast your mind back to 1978. Ferryside complex now, which a long time ago our residential course experience. Glad to report, hairdryer now tamed, actually even better, as totally obliterated!

Health and safety or modernisation has a place, I suppose.

Nothing replaces the old memory of
laughter galore.
Thank you Martin, as old memory brings in
the now chuckles of content.

Bubbles

Pithy person spits her words.
Get out of my head!
FURIOUS without the 'F' word.
Classy lady gives warning.
Beware, next time, tongue lashing 'F' 'F' 'F!
Who or what qualifies the term swearing?
Swearing words or not, tone takes lead.
Increased threat by the silent, sickly, sweet
swearer.
This akin to sugar and diabetes.
Is there concern or need to care?
Crystal clear bubbles or concealed cursing?
Bubbles made to burst.
Words filtered, suggesting angry no more.
Angry, not angry, or on the fence?
Prickly, defensive, but real.
Pretence, welcomed or not?
Politeness, white lies, now let me think.
Pretence, politeness both befitting and real.
Are you true to self and others?
Careful with what you say, otherwise jail
time.
Be free, this is but a game.
Bubbling trail of words energised in
motion.

Beautiful bubbles burst.
Bubbles, mine and yours, offers no
permanence.
Our creator's vision, divinely perfect view
of bubbles.
Chuckling witty exasperation of 'oh dear',
'oh dear'.
Recognition of man, woman and child's
opportunity to make, blow, and burst
bubbles.
Potentials of perfect disallowed at the hand
of human beings,
People, power or poverty?

Bucket, Surf, Castle

Kick the bucket not.
Roar your stuff surf.
Wild woman rides with spirit,
kick not the sand castle.
Respect the child's creation.
What, built by an adult?
Step to the side I say.
Child is king of the castle.

Cried

I prayed for lone criers.
I sensed.
I cried.
Even healing tears needs boosting.
Being with someone crying,
a privilege.
Don't rush to hand the tissues.
Let the healing, cleansing tears,
trickle their loss.
Please, no rushing in,
to offer befitting words.
Trust knowing the power of your presence.
Don't take away by offering more.
Know the power of your presence.
Thank you.
May I have a virtual hug?
Can I gift you with my hug?
Hugging.

Mother Earth says come cwtch with me.
My blanket is big enough for us all.
When you suffer, so do I.
As a mother within all of creation,
I witness your pain, fear and loss.
Shh now – wipe your tears,

gently release your fear.
Make the pain worthwhile,
turning the loss into gain.
I am fine, but people you have work to do.
As I lift my blanket,
I let go and trust.
You are now ready to walk a different path.
I once more ease into rhythmic
beat of love,
now believing you know the truth,
of unconditional love.

Dottie Ty Ni
(Dottie from Our house)

My English teacher approaches me.
She wears an earnest expression, with an
accompanied intense frown.
"Louise," she says in a steady non quivering
voice, "I want you to write a story for the
school eisteddfod."
Teacher's eyes peer over her solid, black-
rimmed glasses with purposeful intent.
Energetically an offering of confidence,
eagerly supporting me to say YES.
Be at the library at 1pm.
Glaring eyes of disbelief.
Upturned noses, as if met with a whiff
pungently uninviting.
Faces of disapproval as my presence
seemingly from the "just above the
twps.-sort of average person" who has
accidentally been dredged up.
From the 'elite sniggering chorus,' a bitchy
girl asks me, "Would you like directions
back to your CLASSroom?"
Sweaty, pimply and a flush of fluster.
"God, please allow me to be swallowed up,
and out of sight."

Ground remains still, with no escape offered.
Musty smell of books entices, with a momentary distraction.
Teacher smiles, seemingly satisfied, as her boosting words of confidence applied, enabled my sense of 'less than worthy, rightful place to write,' has been conquered.
Definitely, NO held high head, from a place of earned respect.
Nervously seated, having been guided by the teacher's commanding firm hand.
Eyes of glazed glare, penetrating my flesh.
Soul says, pick up the pen and write.
Dancing thoughts from the halls of imagination,
I'm lost within rhythmic variables of the gliding pen.
Ecstatic, free as creating something so alive, from cascading ripples of words, until story told.
Writing, my therapist and friend of playfulness, akin to an essential thriving organ.
Spirited, with no hint of distraction from the considered elite pupils, all around me.
Powerful fear, be gone!

I've escaped into the journey of endless possibilities.
Delighted mind engaging with pen and paper.
A story to be told, with a beginning, middle and end.
Possibly rebellion towards structure, with an offering with a difference? Crescendo of rapidity as the wave crashes with breath of satisfaction, as story completed.
Mind, body and soul, working together.
Eisteddfod day.
I'm sitting with a yearning. A desire for my story to be placed within reach of a prize.
"Dottie Ty Ni," is called out.
To my cousin seated beside me, I whisper, "I think that is me."
I hesitated too long, as next my name is called, "Louise Bretland."
My Dulais team members tap my back, pushing me forward towards the stage.
Loud clapping and shouts of, "That's first prize, full points."
A red ribbon is pinned to my bottle green uniform top.
Adrenalin surges through my body.
A joyous result, with proud adorning of the

respected red ribbon.
First prize. Head held high. No gloating, as
writing has greater dignity, from a place of
honourable character.

Eggs of Hope

Three eggs ready to hatch.
You are all needed say eggs.
Within you, me and all of us reality,
a divine essence of powerful hope.
Taking turns, claiming blessings
of being symbolic nests, eggs and birds.

Brooding hope in capital letters.
Feathers within flock create majestic wings
to fly within all tomorrows.
Together in flight we can do this.
Dare to soar within wings of winning ways.
People of power creating newness.

Three eggs, with messages, waiting to be
born.
Life and flight of delight.
Hope, heart, and harmony.
Nests of taking turns in trust.
In flight, rest or nurturing within give and
take.
Trust yourself and trust others.
Allowing broken trust to heal within hearth
of home.

Balanced work, rest and play a must.
Out of control worldwide despair
needs us all to be healers of hope.
Needing to take turns to offer and receive.
Respectful, peaceful ways that judges not
self or others.
Soothing suckles of sincerity.
Sparks of splendour, breathing rekindled
flames of kindness.
Each feather of life in togetherness taking
turn to rest or take flight.

Be your own messenger of hope.
Only then you can earn the right to
encourage others,
as coming from the place of knowing.
Flocking together in flames of flight
that lights the way for evermore,
that needs no full stops.

Emergency visit

Emergency visit which left me without assessment or a triage nurse simply having a look at me, (should happen with all heart patients) because Schizophrenia wrongly documented in my medical notes. They presumed I was having a panic attack due to being mentally ill. Nobody took the time to see in the notes, that at that same hospital I had been an inpatient twice on the cardiology ward. My notes would have a record of my history of needing emergency procedures to address a heart problem. This experience in A & E in 2016 was traumatic for Karl. My potentially life-threatening position which eventually resulted in - emergency treatment, but my signs and symptoms less distressing than witnessing my husband's shock, fear and hurt. This confirmed my truth about clouding of professional opinions still occurring, and medical inequality for people with a psychiatric history. The G.P. letter being needed to support my basic need to gain dignified care with equality, and to be taken seriously in this day and age, is seriously concerning. I don't need to say anymore as the GP letter speaks for itself, as I consider that A&E experience for Karl and me. As I read over the G.P. letter Karl and myself keep on us in hope of safeguarding my care system experiences as a patient, but person first, and as a retired nurse and welfare worker, I feel sad.

Blackbird

Indeed male
I respect your voice.
A song so serene
that awakens passion from beauty.
Chorus not needed
as you alone
do the trick
in my now moment
listening to you.

Male blackbirds more beautiful in
appearance I'm told.
I get it.
But where does that take the concept
of beauty in the eye of the beholder?
Are you unique in your umbrella-
recognition
of comparison
to other male blackbirds
seemingly all the same?

Birds once unnamed to human life
needed not to be qualified with a term
or named identity.
Ignorance can be blissful

as imagination and authenticity
breed with nature
before manmade schools
bombard with strategic curriculums,
timetables;
named life and concepts
to validate and qualify us as real
A lion doesn't need to say it's a lion to be a
lion.
Something wise someone once shared
from a philosophical
someone else's words and not mine,
but this I like as deeply but simply true.

Blackbird,
the background of green so deep
and red flaming berries
enrich your centre-stage
sharing your song effortlessly
all with such ease.
But needing to be vigilant
as freedom or total security
devoid of harm or attack
available to you Blackbird,
me or anyone else
not true.

Knowing there is no freedom
time to call in the dove of peace,
knowing wisdom needed
as there is never total peace.
This is freedom.

Mothers

Mother Earth.
Goddess of Nature.
Mother Gaia.
So much more than within your naming.
Your womb so fertile.
Sexual intercourse not needed.
From chaos of nothingness, you uniquely
create life.
Mother to us all, being your daughter I
honour and claim.

Mammy, my biological mother, I love you.
Your passing in 2008, to the heavenly life
chapter.
Our human minds harbour an array of
perceptions.
Does life continue, after earthly time
apparently ends, or not?
Your ashes in 2020, still waiting to be
returned to Mother Earth.
Your golden wedding ring still on Earth.
I want to let you know I understand.
No more needs to be said, as energies
cleared with wisdom gained.
I embrace forgiveness towards myself and

others.
You are love, Mammy, and my love ripples into love, love, love.

I am a non-official mother, adorning an apron so homely.
My apron pockets of plenty, so deep.
No frills or pretence I offer you.
2019, my womb, tubes, ovaries and other bits surgically taken.
I wish soon after, a Cwtch- a hug from a fellow known female of trust, had been available.
I was never blessed with having my own babies to carry, birth, or nurture.
Knowing I have been privileged to be a non-biological mother, to so many.
No womb, no babies, but mother source of truth.
I am still Mother in my eyes, and that witnessed sometimes by others.
Many blind eyes, refusing to see my role of mother representation.
Have I the earned right to represent mother of any kind?

People are people.

Wombs are wombs.
Birth is birth.
So much learnt from prejudice, ignorance, stigma and so much more.
All the negatives and beautiful, beautiful positives, all equal.
We as people not as in control and in charge as we think.
Do you have the courage to still trust without any specifics, or guarantees?
Can you feel and embrace the trust?
Are you able to grant this trust to Mother Earth, source, or whatever our creator means to you?
If owning true faith, already you will know that never will you walk your path alone.
Are you and I consumers of sufficient humble pies?
Have life's pies nourished me in ways enabling me to feed other lives, in meaningful ways?
Pure white light of a power greater than I, please guide me to be the best that I can, in my I am.

Bird's Nest, Flowers
and Mamgu's Cwtch

Eggs going to hatch any day. Oh damn, my
Wellington boot stuck in muddy hole, Pull-
oops nearly fell on bum! Mamgu doesn't
like muddy socks, | mustn't wipe my dirty
hands on my dress, Touching eggs and nest
not allowed. Is the mother bird watching
me like Mamgu said? | mustn't stay too long
as the bird needs to get back to her eggs
and keep them warm. Grown-ups say that
cold eggs mean no chicks, Beautiful blue
corn flower. Blue is my favourite colour.
Walking through the green grass with
Mamgu, learning all the flower names.
This we call our meadow gifts place, Happy
colours with cheerful flower faces, makes
Mamgu and me smile, Cwtch times with
Mamgu is special on the big fat sofa and
cushions smelling of apple pies, Mamgu's
arms wrapped around me. Feeling safe and
warm inside with tingles all over my body.
Sharing stories together while watching
the dancing orange and yellow flames. Do
the chicks feel like this when their Mum
cwtched them with her soft tummy feathers
and keep safe wings? Mamgu says 'yes'.

I Can Be Me.

No time to be a patient.
Please let's work together.
I need to and I must be a patient,
So the person in me can thrive.

Not being listened to.
Wanting to listen to others for the right
reasons.
I need to be heard.
Trust me as I trust myself.

I am an adult in a child's world.
I am an adult, even when my
communication
seems childlike.
People ask yourselves
are you being the adult for you.

Not paying for cake
I have paid for my cake,
no payment required.
I am offering you some of my cake,
offering, not asking.

Checking the scar.

See beyond clinical.
Seeing the person and trusting the value
gained.
A scar represents a life lived,
valuing the scar, like a star.

Is Louise going to die?
Maybe she is, but possibly needlessly
if people don't stop and think,
so that we can all be heard accurately.
Basics.

I can be me.
I am me.
People relax and trust me being me.
Welcoming safe support as I am vulnerable.
I am me.

I can be me.

No Fixed Abode

The atlas guiding my brain,
The atlas guiding my brain, says no to
singing.
Ataxia the thief. Sobs of 'hiraeth-longing,'
knowing singing days over. Needing to cry,
here and there, but not in stuck ways.
Singing
my soul medicine. Soul smiles knowingly,
as spoken voice, still truly nourishing.
Acceptance created with willingness.
Timing has no clock reality. Daringly
seeking
new ways. This not easy but remains a
choice.
Cleansing, healing tears, thank you.
Inviting in more
and more, with gratitude, the welcoming of
my spoken
voice. A journey of trust, with no promises.
Life geared by
choices, owns the version of what was, is, or
to be. Ego
respected, but asked to step back. My voice
can speak
with courage, with good humour, and

laughter. Letting go
not easy, but gained enough wisdom, to
grasp this needs
investment, otherwise, ego crushes further
my soul.
Speaking up, has a louder voice, than my
ego. Respecting
ego's role, but told firmly its place, being the
backing vocalist.

Hiraeth

Un ton ar ol ton o hiraeth.
Anal byr a fas rhwng tonnau cryf.
Perygl o foddi yn llifogydd o dagrau.
Rhegi a poeri allan y poen
gyda'r gair damio drosodd a drosodd.
Byth rhagor yr un peth.
Dim yn bosibl anghofio
pobl cariadus neu cofion cynnes.
Fy nghalon dynner yn rhwygo
gyda ergyd trwm i'm ysbryd.
Hiraeth yw'r gair na gall fod yn llai.
Teimlad ofnadwy yn bwrw eich enaid,
dyna ystyr hiraeth.
Cymro neu Cymraes
wedi canu sawl emyn mewn angladd
i ddeall dwfnder y gair hiraeth.

Longing

One wave after wave of longing.
Short shallow breath,
between each powerful wave.
Danger of drowning, in floods of tears.
Swearing and spitting out the pain,
with the word damn over and over.
Never again to be the same.
Impossible to forget loving people,
or warm memories.
My tender heart rips,
with a heavy impact to my spirit.
Longing, a word that cannot be less.
A terrible feeling that hits the soul,
that's the meaning of longing.
Welshman or Welsh woman,
having sung several hymns at a funeral,
will understand the depth of the word
longing.

Acknowledgements

My thanks to:

People Speak Up Founder and Artistic Director, Eleanor Shaw and her amazing team, and fellow group participants at PSU.

Mel Perry and Dominic Williams, Directors of write4word.

Skanda Vale Hospice team, and particularly Kate Pawsey who was volunteering her professional role MSc as a practitioner of 'Creative Writing for Therapeutic Purposes.'

For the love and dedicated support from my husband, Stephen Karl Treharne, and our departed dogs Alfie top dog, and Will Bach, and our now beautiful dog Gwen, the whole package!

Working with Plant Dewi, supported by People Speak Up, this an exciting project that not only captures some of the most neglected superheroes of the pandemic, but it also honours and celebrates motherhood and ramps up resilience, through creativity and empowerment. It allows mothers to testify to the times, for their voices and stories to be honoured, elevated and take up space in language and literature.

The publisher gratefully acknowledges the financial support of Literature Wales and the Royal College of Psychiatrists.